Rural Land Reform, Peasants' Rights and the Collective Economy:

Three Major Issues in China Agricultural Development

Li Zhou and Ren Changqing
Translated by Li Yanqing

Pi Paths International Ltd

中国社会科学出版社
CHINA SOCIAL SCIENCES PRESS

Abstract: The fact of continuous steady agricultural growth for more than three decades in China shows that, the collective ownership of rural land has flexibility and inclusiveness, its ambiguous negative impact is limited. The constantly improved realization form of collective ownership of rural land facilitates land exchange, transfer and consolidation. The rural land property right reform aims to further improve the property right structure of collective land ownership, the most appropriate method is to manifest the implicit land equity. Stocklization of rural land is helpful to solve the sidelining of agriculture and land fragmentation issues, could increase the flexibility of land occupation and transfer, the efficiency of land utilization and the competitiveness of agriculture. Stock ownership of rural land has strong stability, may be defined by warrants. Management right of rural land is flexible, may be divided and merged, and should be defined by contracts.

Rural land transfer is the rational choice of peasants and the result of market allocation of resources, government should not intervene. Government should substitute land planning management system for land acquisition system, bring the decisive role of market allocation of resources into play by establishing an open, competitive, unified and orderly land market. Innovate realization forms for the usufructuary right of peasant house sites and peasant housing property right, set the bottom line for transfer of housing property right, guarantee housing security of the peasants. Rural land transaction system serves some collective economic organizations and peasants, yet rural land protection and management system serves all collective economic organizations and peasant households, so rural land protection and management system should be designed with priority.

Advocating the development of collective economy intends to solve the backwardness of collective economy development, not to suppress the existance of other economic sectors. The development of collective economy should not follow the old way of "gathering" and evil ways of depriving the peasants, but should find a new way of members with equal rights, co-ownership of assets by shares, performance-based interest sharing, relying on the peasants and serving the peasants. The peasants should decide the cooperation mode jointly, design the supervision and incentive system jointly, this is the basis to increase collective action performance and guarantee healthy development of collective economy. Transit from able person model to institutional model by returning the property ownership to people, giving power to people, improving systems, optimizing control, strengthening management and normalizing operation.

Keywords: collective ownership of rural land, rural land transfer, peasants' rights and interests, collective economy

Contents

1. Insistence on collective ownership of rural land 1
1.1 The changes of land issues in rural reform 2
1.1.1 The contracted management right of collective land 2
1.1.2 Transfer right of the lands contracted by peasant households 4
1.1.3 Property right of collective land 5
1.2 Issues in the collective ownership of rural land 6
1.3 Theoretical basis of insistence on collective ownership of rural land and the suggestions for countermeasures 8
1.3.1 The reason of collective ownership of rural land 8
1.3.2 The meaning of collective ownership of rural land 9
1.3.3 Theoretical explanation of the collective ownership of rural land 10
1.3.4 Institutional framework for the collective ownership of rural land 14
1.3.5 Direction of the collective ownership of rural land 16
1.3.6 Suggestions for countermeasures against adjusting the realization form of collective ownership of rural land 17

2. Safeguard the peasants' rights and interests in land according to law 20
2.1 Evaluation of the policy for rights and interests in rural land 20
2.1.1 Policy deviation that influences the rights and interests of rural collective economic organizations 22
2.1.2 Deviation of the peasants' excessive exercise of rights and interests in land caused by loose management 23
2.1.3 Evaluation of the government land policy 24
2.2 Safeguard the peasants' rights and interests in land according to law 25
2.2.1 Safeguard collective ownership of rural land according to law 26
2.2.2 Normalize the behaviors of government and officials according to law 26

2.2.3 Normalize the behaviors of village cadres according to law 26
2.2.4 Improve the laws and regulations to safeguard peasants' rights and interests in land 26
2.3 Policy suggestions for safeguarding the peasants' rights and interests in land 27
2.3.1 Change rural land from physical capital to equity capital 27
2.3.2 Promote the reform of rural collective land shareholding system 28
2.3.3 Optimization of macropolicy environment for land system reform 29

3. Development of collective economy 30
3.1 The significance of developing collective economy 30
3.1.1 Analysis of the influencing factors of collective action performance 30
3.1.2 Analysis on the necessity and possibility of developing rural collective economy 32
3.1.3 The reason of slow development of rural collective economy 34
3.1.4 Favorable conditions for the development of collective economy 35
3.2 Legal status of rural collective economic organizations 36
3.2.1 Optimize the development environment of collective economic organizations from the improvement of relevant laws and regulations 36
3.2.2 Quicken the legislation of rural collective economic organizations 37
3.2.3 Legislative suggestions 38
3.3 Overall thinking and policy suggestions for the development of rural collective economy 38
3.3.1 Overall thinking 38
3.3.2 Policy suggestions 40
3.3.3 Tendencies to be prevented 40

1. Insistence on collective ownership of rural land

It is defined in the Constitution of China that: "Land in the rural and suburban areas is owned by collectives except for those portions which belong to the state in accordance with the law; house sites and privately farmed plots of cropland and hilly land are also owned by collectives. "

Collective ownership of rural land is not only stipulated in law, but is also the universal recognition of peasants. For more than three decades, hundreds of millions of peasants have basically never questioned the existing rural land system, nor there is any reaction of disagreement. The questioning in reality is actually the idea of some scholars.

At the economic development stage of small average household management scale, no matter in promoting modern agriculture, enhancing agricultural competitiveness and sustainable development level, or reducing the conflicts in dual economy transformation process, collective ownership of land has its advantage over private ownership of land. Just because of this advantage, China becomes a main body of agricultural labor transfer, rather than a country of bankrupt peasants.

The collective ownership of rural land in China has very strong flexibility and inclusiveness in the realize form. Such flexibility and inclusiveness allows the property right structure of collective land to be adjusted correspondingly to meet the productivity growth requirements. Ambiguity also exists in the collective ownership of rural land in China, however, negative impact of such ambiguity is restricted. The reason for this judgment: it is impossible for an unrealistic ownership system of rural land to maintain steady growth of China's agriculture for over 30 years. Therefore, we should have confidence in the existing rural land system, rather than denying this system hastily.

1.1 The changes of land issues in rural reform

The changes of rural land issues since the reform in China must be analyzed in combination with the course of rural reform, rather than discussion only on lands. The cause and effect of land issues may be made clear with practical and realistic attitude, the methods or solutions may thus be found to solve these issues only when such issues are put in rural reform environment.

At the early stage of reform, in order to meet the demand of peasants for adequate food and clothing, the central government recognized the practice initiated by peasants, i.e. "all-round responsibility system" gradually. Thus, peasants achieved independent labor right in the "all-round responsibility system". Collective economic organizations award the contract of land management right to peasant households in the principle of fair, this is the prerequisite to implement independent labor right of the peasants. After the demand for adequate food and clothing is met, in order to meet the demand of the peasants to go out for non-agricultural employment, the central government entitles the peasants to transfer their land management right independently. The diversified forms of land transfer in reality are specific practices to implement such empowerment. Now, in order to meet demand of the peasants to safeguard their land property right, the central government should empower land shares to the peasants; define stock ownership of collective land possessed by peasant households in the forms of right vertification, stock verification and issuance of warrants, this is also a specific practice to implement the reform objectives: co-ownership of the property right of rural collective land by shares.

1.1.1 The contracted management right of collective land

Demand of the peasants for adequate food and clothing could not be solved for a long time, it became the blasting fuse of rural reform at the end of the 1970s. At that time, peasants universally thought that, commune members were forced to work together, yet nobody could determine the quantity and quality of work done by each member clearly; the system of "getting an equal share regardless of the work done", tied down their production enthusiasm. With respect to this problem, an innovative way of collective agricultural production and management, called "all-round responsibility system" appeared. The so-called "all-round responsibility system" means the contracting of collective lands (rights) and agricultural output (responsibilities) on these lands, doing own work. This is an institutional arrangement with symmetrical rights and obligations, neither the responsibility system nor the contracted management right may be emphasized unilaterally.

At that time, peasants claimed the right of independent labor, rather than the right of land possession. Reason of this judgment: in "all-round responsibility system", peasants do not participate in collective labor any more, after deducting the predefined grain tax to the state and the amount retained by the collective, the rest fruits of labor are owned by the peasants and may be distributed by the peasants independently. Compared with the people's commune system, only collective labor and collective distribution links are omitted. It is the lands and works of collective economic organizations that are contracted in the "all-round responsibility system", and this is its significant feature distinguished from "single production in seperate fields", also the main judgment basis of collective ownership of land unchanged due to "all-round responsibility system". It should be pointed out that, not only "all-round responsibility system" policy empowers independent labor right to peasants, the policy of departing farming without leaving native land also empowers independent labor right to the peasants, i.e. the right of peasants not to be engaged in agriculture. The difference lies in: the former empowers the peasants to be engaged in agriculture independently, the latter empowers the peasants to be engaged in non-agricultural employment independently.

It should be mentioned that, the ownership and management right of collective lands belong to collective economic organizations in "all-round responsibility system", institutional arrangement of co-ownership of the property right of collective land by shares does not exist yet. At that time, peasant households got the right to contract the management right of collective land, rather than the right to contract ownership of collective land. The right to contract and the management right are two rights. A predefined part of the fruits of the peasants' labor is retained by collective economic organizations, this embodies the rights and interests for the transfer of management right of collective land. Because the ownership of collective land is not transferred, so collective economic organizations do not obtain the rights and interests of land ownership. This is the same as the function of interest, which is the rights and interests for management right of capital, rather than the rights and interests of capital ownership.

In a few words, it is the independent labor right that is empowered to peasants at the early stage of reform. Collective economic organizations award the contract of management right of collective land to peasants in the principle of fair, this is a specific practice to implement the independent labor right of peasants, arouse production enthusiasm of the peasants. "All-round responsibility system" is an institutional arrangement with symmetrical rights and obligations. Collective economic organizations award the contract of management right of collective land in the principle of fair, get the rights and interests of management right of collective land by retaining. Peasants do not obtain the right to contract and the management right of collective land simultaneously.

1.1.2 Transfer right of the lands contracted by peasant households

Demand of the peasants for adequate food and clothing was met very quickly after “all-round responsibility system” was enforced. This shows that, independent labor of the peasants is really effective to meet the demand for adequate food and clothing. After the demand for adequate food and clothing is met, disadvantages of such ultra-small scale agricultural management mode that restricts the application of new technology and the development of modern agriculture are exposed. Thankfully, the continuous rapid development of Chinese economy, brings about non-agricultural employment opportunities of more and more posts, more and more stability for the peasants. Continuous increase of the peasants’ employment structure enables non-agricultural employment a main source of the peasant households to increase their income on the one hand, and increases the opportunity cost of being engaged in agricultural production gradually on the other hand. Since some peasant households are reluctant to take agriculture as a sideline, land transfer behavior appears among peasant households. The transfer of contracted land is favorable to overcome the disadvantges of ultra-small scale agricultural management, promote the application of new agricultural technology, push the development of modern agriculture, so the transfer of lands contracted by peasant households basically encounters no obstacle. Transfer of the contracted land seems like a natural right.

As a whole, total quantity of the contracted lands to be transferred out by peasant households is less than the total quantity of contracted lands to be transferred in by peasant households, this means that the development speed of appropriate management scale could not meet the demand of farmers. The intervention of other entities (for example, companies) further intensifies the short supply in the transfer market of contracted lands. This is largely why organizational transfer fee of contracted lands is increased year after year. Therefore, the real agricultural situation in China: number of peasant households willing to take ultra-small scale agriculture as a sideline does not decrease fast enough, peasant households that are willing to expand management scale could hardly meet their desired targets. With more and more peasant households waiving ultra-small scale agriculture, sideline agriculture will be lack of successors; while farmers will become main body of the agriculture in China with more and more of them meeting their desired targets step by step.

1.1.3 Property right of collective land

With more and more peasant households transferring their contracted lands out, and the emerging of more and more transfer forms, larger and larger total scale being transferred out, the existing rural land property arrangements could no longer meet the requirements. Because, if a member of a collective economic organization only has the contracted management right of collective land, then he loses the connection with collective land ownership once he transfers the management right of his contracted land out. If that's true, then the more actively the land management right is transferred out, the more complicated, and more uncontrollable the member composition of collective land ownership becomes.

The existing argument is that, members of a rural collective economic organization possess the right to contract land and the land management right, but they only transfer the management right out, they still hold the right to contract land. Such argument is worth discussing. As mentioned above, peasants obtained independent labor right in "all-round responsibility system", rather than obtaining three rights simultaneously, i.e. independent labor right, land contract right and land management right. For the issues arising from land transfer, we should not try to find new interpretation in the original property right structure, but should further improve the existing property right structure.

In order to keep stability of the members in a rural collective economic organization, enable transfer of land management right to be more and more active, the most appropriate method is to manifest the implicit land equity. Members of a collective economic organization obtaining the right to contract actually rely on their possession of collective land stock ownership. Rural collective economy was developed in the form of peasants converting their lands into shares in the 1950s. As it were, it is logical to manifest and embody the implicit, fuzzy stock ownership.

Three advantages may be achieved to manifest the collective land stock ownership: firstly, claims of the members of a collective economic organization for collective land ownership may be protected by law, and stability of the members in collective economic organization may be maintained. Secondly, the problem of peasants losing their relationship with collective land once they transfer management right of the contracted land out may be solved effectively. Thirdly, subject of land transfer may be normalized. The rights and interests of land management right are limited, in order to reduce the subject participating in distribution, the following provisions must be observed: only collective economic organization and the members of collective economic organization who possess collective land equity have the right to transfer their disposable land management right. The land management right obtained from transfer could not be transferred further to other operation bodies, so as to prevent the transfer of land management right again and again, and prevent a broker group living on the transfer of land management right.

Stock ownership of rural collective land is unchanged for a long time, has very strong stability, should be defined by warrants. Management right of rural collective land is often changed, has extremely strong flexibility, it should be defined by contract. Members of a collective economic organization with collective land stock certificate (equivalent to property ownership certificate) may use their own collective land management right, may also transfer all or part of their collective land management right to lessees for use, here, collective land stock certificate (property ownership certificate) is still in their hands. The rights and interests of peasant households to transfer their land management right is generally positive. However, facing the policy of no idle rural land for years, peasant households might also accept negative result of the rights and interests for transferring out their management right to protect their land equity.

After a collective economic organization issues land stock certificate to its members, the ownership of collective land still belongs to the members of collective economic organization jointly, it is indivisible. Collective land equity is distributed within the qualified collective economic organization members in the principle of fairness, so as to realize co-ownership of the collective land by shares. Peasant household with land stock certificate is the smallest and most important subject to participate in the transfer of land management right, but not the only subject. Collective action of the peasant households with land stock certificate is helpful to reduce the transfer cost of land management right, and helpful to find out the demander of land management right with stronger operation capability at higher price, helpful to increase competitiveness of the agriculture market in China. Of course, this is completely voluntary collective action of peasant households. This shows that, ownership of collective land is an integral whole,while stock ownership and management right of collective land may be divided and merged.

1.2 Issues in the collective ownership of rural land

At the early stage of reform, "three deductions and five charges" was the realization form of collective ownership of rural land. It was not only the economic realization form of collective ownership of rural land, but also the prerequisite to develop public goods supply capacity. Unfortunately, such theoretically self-justifying practice was criticized due to problems in practical operation. Affected by a series of extreme cases, such problems were amplified to such an extent that turmoil might occur in rural areas if it was not repealed. So, the government cancelled agricultural tax, implemented equal basic public services in urban and rural areas, issued subsidies to village cadres and so on, eliminated the opportunity of collecting "three deductions and five charges" by levying agricultural tax from collective economic organizations. In case rural collective economic organizations could no longer acquire rights and interests from management right of the contracted land through "three deductions and five charges", ownership and management right of collective land are separated thoroughly: collective economic organization reserves the dummy ownership, peasant households obtain complete land management right. It is no secret that, this practice pushes rural land property right towards privatization one step further. The right verification that defines four boundaries and area of the lands contracted by peasant households pushes rural land property right towards privatization another step further on this basis.

Objectively speaking, the viewpoint on public ownership and private ownership of land is mainly affected by ideology, rather than a scientific conclusion. Reason of this judgment: number of countries that implement private ownership of rural land is far more than the number of countries that develop agriculture successfully in the world; developing countries that implement private ownership of rural land hardly develop agriculture successfully; the agricultural development case in China is insufficient to reach the conclusion of collective land ownership superior to private land ownership. However, we should not advocate collective ownership ideologically, yet promote private land ownership on policy orientation.

Looking back, the conflict between peasants and village cadres caused by "three deductions and five charges" is not a global issue. Government has one-sidedness in denying "three deductions and five charges" system from top to bottom to alleviate the burden of peasants. Firstly, in developed areas, the "three deductions and five charges" to be deducted by collective economic organization is generally assumed by township and village enterprises, furious conflict between peasants and village cadres caused by "three deductions and five charges" does not exist in these areas. Secondly, "three deductions and five charges" in other villages is mostly done according to the provisions of the government, furious conflict between peasants and village cadres because of it does not exist. Thirdly, for existing problems, solution should be found by analyzing genesis of the problems, rather than putting the problems aside, yet repealing "three deductions and five charges" system from top to bottom. In a few words, the government substitutes fiscal transfer payment system for "three deductions and five charges" system, overemphasizes "three deductions and five charges" aggravating the burden of peasants, yet neglectes "three deductions and five charges" as the realization form of collective ownership. Such practice that deprives collective economic organizations of exercising legitimate rights from top to bottom, belongs to a nudge in the wrong direction. This is a lesson we must learn.

1.3 Theoretical basis of insistence on collective ownership of rural land and the suggestions for countermeasures

1.3.1 The reason of collective ownership of rural land

(1) A household could not be engaged in production independently

At the beginning of mankind, initial production unit was clan commune rather than household. At this long historical stage, land was owned collectively. Main reason of collective land ownership was that it's difficult for a household to become independent production unit. This type of collective land ownership has no intersection with existing collective ownership of rural land in China, so it is unworthy of more textual research.

(2) Ideological preference

It is no secret that, changing of private land ownership to collective ownership in the 1950s was partially for implementing catching-up strategy in China, and partially for ideological reasons. At that time, mainstream socialist economic theory thought that, public ownership of the means of production was essential characteristic of socialist economic system. Considering the national circumstances in which agriculture was dominant in the economic structure, public ownership of rural land became the key to establish public ownership of the means of production. At that time, academic discussions were carried out surrounding a grand proposition, how to realize the ultimate goal of communists more quickly. These discussions were far away from actual situation of rural productivity and economic base in China, basically of no meaning on improving the collective ownership of rural land in China, also unworthy of more textual research.

(3) Defects of market mechanism

In the market economy with imperfect mechanism, insufficient competition and asymmetric information, the peasant households take cooperation as a strategy of equal transaction with industrial and commercial capital. This is why peasants' cooperation appeared in the developed countries very long ago, and why agricultural cooperatives in these countries were incorporated with the improvement of market mechanism. Peasants' cooperation does not mean collective land ownership, however, the experience developed in this process is of reference signification for improving collective ownership of rural land in China, so it is worth doing systematic processing and textual research.

(4) Innovation of development pattern

Some scholars in China have developed a mind-set to follow the way of developed countries, never consider any better alternative pattern, they deny institutional arrangement of collective ownership of rural land on these grounds. The facts in Russia and Eastern European countries where they have taken radical reform strategy for transformation to the development pattern of developed countries as soon as possible, yet haven't achieved success in economic development up to the present show that, the development pattern of developed countries is not universally applicable; the facts of successful economic development in China, Vietnam and other countries where progressive reform strategy is taken to explore the development pattern suitable to solve their own problems show that, great potential exists for the innovation of development pattern.

For more than 30 years since the reform and opening, remarkable achievements have been obtained in the economic development of China. Chinese approach, Chinese model and Chinese system have been accepted by more and more people. Chinese scholars have the liabilities and conditions to sort out and summarize the innovations in the development patterns, modules or elements of successful practices. We should not belittle ourselves improperly in this aspect, nor imitate others and thus lose our own individuality, follow in the footsteps of other countries passively.

1.3.2 The meaning of collective ownership of rural land

(1) Ideological view

The collective ownership of rural land is advocated in China, in addition to the most important material base of collective economic organizations, collective ownership of rural land is also deemed as an important component of socialist public ownership ideologically.

(2) Legal view

It is specified in Article 8 of the Organic Law of the Villagers Committees in China that: villagers committee should manage the land and other properties collectively owned by the villagers in this village according to law, guide villagers to utilize natural resources reasonably, protect and improve eco-environment. It is specified in Article 13 of the Law on Land Contract in Rural Areas of China: the contract-issuing party (i.e. the villagers committee) enjoys the following rights: award contract of the rural land that is owned by this collective or owned by the State, yet used by this collective according to law; supervise the contractor to utilize and protect the land reasonably according to the contractual purpose; inhibit any behavior of the contractor to destroy the contracted land and agricultural resources.

(3) Path dependence view

Two-level management system with the combination of centralization and decentralization, incentive compatibility is implemented for agriculture in China. Main responsibility of collective management organization is to provide public goods and services. Insist on collective ownership of rural land, develop collective economy, safeguard community identity, enhance villagers cohesion, promote villagers' mutual aid.

(4) Responsibility sharing view

With respect to the supply of public goods for rural communities, besides government, more and more large households in the village assume greater responsibilities, but as a whole, peasant households assume more responsibilities jointly. Insistence on collective land ownership and development of collective economy is the foundation for peasant households to assume responsibilities jointly. So the appropriate practices: restore three deductions (public accumulation funds, public welfare fund and overhead expenses) system, improve "case-by-case" system. For these two systems, government should play the role of complementation rather than substitution.

1.3.3 Theoretical explanation of the collective ownership of rural land

Theoretical explanation of the collective ownership of rural land varies with the understanding of socialist system. Before reform and opening, collective ownership of rural land was a prerequisite to promote the agricultural production system "large in size and collective in nature". With respect to the relations of production, collective ownership of rural land embodies essential characteristics of socialism, and is the primary form of public ownership, it will be transited to advanced form of public ownership, i.e. ownership by the whole people gradually. With respect to productivity, large scale agricultural production on the basis of socialist public ownership is used to overcome large scale agricultural production on the basis of capitalist private ownership. Essential differences between two economic systems are emphasized here.

Since the reform and opening, research emphasis changes from outlining an ambitious goal to solving practical problems. Although the argues on collective ownership of rural land and ownership by peasant households still exist occasionally (see Special Column 1) , yet there are less and less participants, social influence becomes smaller and smaller. As a whole, scholars no longer care the essential differences between socialist economic system and capitalist economic system, but how to bring the role of market mechanism on the basis of socialist public ownership into full play, expand inclusiveness of socialist economic system continuously.

(1) The relationship between collective ownership of rural land and the economic system reform goal in China

The goal of economic transformation in China is to establish socialist market economic system with Chinese characteristics. This goal has three keywords. Firstly, Chinese characteristics. It emphasizes endogenesis, i.e. developed gradually in the Chinese model itself, rather than something moved from abroad. Secondly, socialist. It emphasizes symbiosis, i.e. Chinese model is a joint development model, rather than a partially developed, partially undeveloped model. Thirdly, market economy. It emphasizes competitive survival, i.e. Chinese model has general characteristics of economic development. Market economic system with endogenesis and symbiosis is a more inclusive system, allows the development of both private economy and collective economy.

> Although collective ownership of rural land is specified in law and is thc common understanding of the peasants, yet scholars still have their own policy claims:
>
> Firstly, the claim of rural land privatization. Scholars with such claim believe that, rural land privatization will enable peasants to be sentimentally attached to land, increase the investment in land, promote scale operation, which is favorable for agricultural and rural development; peasants may obtain funds to go to town by selling land or mortgage to promote urbanization and development of the peasants; rural land privatization could prevent rural collective from infringing peasants' interests, inhibit land enclosure by officials.

Secondly, the claim of immaterializing collective ownership of rural land. Scholars with such claim believe that, private rights of peasants for the contracted land including the rights of use, usufruct and disposition should be strengthened, rights of the collective economic organization or village committee for land adjustment, charging contracting fee etc should be eliminated, so as to immaterialize collective ownership of rural land to an ideological system with co-ownership characteristics.

Thirdly, the claim of subdividing rural land property right. Scholars with such claim believe that, rural land property right needs to be subdivided, ownership belongs to the collective, and the right to contract belongs to peasant households, management right should be assigned to large households, cooperatives and agriculture-related enterprises. The collective obtains management fee, the contracted households obtain land rent and dividends, land operators obtain operating income.

Fourthly, the claim of maintaining collective ownership. Scholars with such claim believe that, before social security system becomes perfect, collective land ownership safeguards the right of the peasants to live, and safeguards the village collective to be able to supply public goods such as irrigation and water conservancy facilities, maintenance of rural road etc.

Data source: Tang Hao: is Collective Ownership of Rural Land Not Required Any More? *Contemporary Economic Research*, 2012(6).

(2) The relationship between collective ownership of rural land and progressive reform strategy in China

Progressive reform strategy is promoted in China. ① Compared with radical reform strategy, progressive reform strategy has two distinctive features.

Firstly, the strategy is relatively mild, does not go to extremes. This is why China tries to correct the biased error of planned economic system instead of getting rid of the planned economic system immediately. Specifically to rural land, collective land ownership with both private factors and public factors is implemented, instead of thorough public ownership or private ownership.

Secondly, the goal advances with times, measures are improved gradually.

① The selection of progressive reform strategy in China is strongly correlated to the politicians promoting the reform, who were the designers and operators of planned economic system. They initiated the reform to overcome the disadvantges of planned economic system, rather than denying the planned economic system thoroughly. In transition countries where radical reform is promoted, the reform is mostly guided by newly elected politicians. They launched radical reform and denied existing system thoroughly, attempted to accomplish the whole task at one stroke, and to meet national psychology of the system in Europe and America being the best system.

The essential of progressive reform strategy in China is to regard economic system transformation as a protracted war, dispose bad cards one by one by deepening the reform continuously, after the bad cards are disposed away, economic development gets on the right track. This is a process of accumulating small victories into great victory. Politicians who highly praise the radical reform strategy believe the theory of quick victory, they adopt the strategy of playing good cards at one time. The problem is that bad cards will not disappear naturally because good cards are played, so the effort of accomplishing the whole task at one stroke usually could not achieve the expected goal. Although the progressive reform strategy implemented in China has achieved results which attracted worldwide attention, yet some scholars still advocate radical reform strategy, they always complain the reform in China not fast enough, not thorough enough. Of course, property right subject is really ambiguous in collective ownership of rural land, yet a conclusion of destroying it as soon as possible could not be reached on these grounds. The real work to do is to deepen the reform, make best use of the advantages and bypass the disadvantages, be more adaptive to the requirements of agricultural development in China.

The scholars who are anxious to destroy collective land ownership often neglect the advantages of such property arrangement. Compared with private land ownership, the advantages of collective ownership of rural land include: firstly, easy land exchange between peasant households. The actually unifrom vegetable greenhouses in rows are the result of land exchange between peasant households. Successful land exchange between peasant households is strongly correlated to collective land ownership. Secondly, easy land transfer. Land transfer in China is obviously faster than that in other economic entities of the East Asia. Quick land transfer is also strongly correlated to collective land ownership. Thirdly, easy linking of pieces of farm lands. This may be realized easily in China, and is also strongly correlated to collective land ownership.

(3) The relationship between collective ownership of rural land and meeting new appeals of the peasants continuously

A remarkable feature of Chinese governance model is to attach importance to the complementarity of efficient market and positive government. To maintain and extend such complementarity, government must hold the power of regulation. Collective ownership of rural land facilitates the government to launch measures to meet new appeals of the peasants, such efficacy is an important reason for the government to insist on collective ownership of rural land. At the early stage of reform, government fully released production enthusiasm of the peasants by meeting their appeals for independent labor, solved the problem of agricultural product supply falling short of demand, met adequate food and clothing demand of the peasants, developed the first complementation between efficient market and positive government. After adequate food and clothing demand was met, government eliminated worries of the peasants parting from agriculture by meeting land transfer appeals of the peasants, promoted the development of industrialization and urbanization, increased the income of peasant households, developed the second complementation between efficient market and positive government. Now, government implements land equity to peasant households by meeting appeals of the peasants to get income from land property in the forms of right vertification, stock verification and issuance of warrants, then implements the reform goal of income right of the peasants from land property and co-ownership of collective land property right by shares, has developed the third complementation between efficient market and positive government. It's not difficult to imagine that, if rural land was privatized, the government is unable to play good cards one by one in a progressive mode. For this, disposal of bad cards one by one and playing good cards one by one in a progressive mode is the most important experience of China in successful reform.

1.3.4 Institutional framework for the collective ownership of rural land

Some scholars think that, collective ownership of rural land is the result of dominant ideology in China. This is surely reasonable, but incomplete. From the viewpoint of inclusive development, centralization of land management right in a few large households, which falls into companies passively must be prevented in case labor market has not been fully developed, rural social security system has not been established completely. Although the existance of collective land ownership and collective economic organizations could not help vulnerable groups that fail temporarily in market competition or peasant households that encounter unforeseeable difficulties to break away from dilemma, yet could provide some help for them to go through a difficult period after all. To put it more bluntly, private land ownership might be the result of economic development in China,yet it is not the precondition of economic development in China, i.e. collective ownership or private ownership of land will become more and more unimportant with the increase of economic development level in China.

Chinese economy is being transited from a developing country to a developed country. Framework of rural land system should have three features at this stage, i.e. stability, flexibility and effectiveness.

(1) Stability

The so-called stability, means that collective members who possess the land of specific community should be stable, will not change easily. For this, firstly, reduce land equity transaction between collective members; secondly, control the land equity transaction scope within the collective members; thirdly, define qualification of the subject which transfers land management right out strictly, i.e. only land equity owner is qualified to transfer land management right out, so as to prevent the impact of transfer for many times on the stability of land property right.

(2) Flexibility

Land property right in physical form is the initial form of property right, however, land property right should not stay in initial form of property right. Compared with land property right in physical form, land property right in equity form is not only favorable for consolidation of fragmented lands, but also favorable for further segmentation of land property right, so land property right in equity form is a more flexible definition mode of property right. Collective ownership of rural land in China initiated from peasants converting their lands into shares to join the commune, now land equity is implemented to collective members in the principle of fairness, land equity that was ambiguous for decades actually becomes clear.

(3) Effectiveness

Here effectiveness refers to overall effectiveness. Including effectiveness of the protection of rights and interests of the collective economic organization and collective members who hold land equity, effectiveness of agricultural production of the land operator, as well as effectiveness of sustainable land use concerned by the state. To achieve effectiveness in these three aspects, a platform must be built, on which the government, market and community (stakeholder group) play their respective roles together. Single market mechanism could not meet the effectiveness requirement in these three aspects simultaneously. The author found during the survey in Korea that, in case lands may be traded freely, the lands purchased by farmers are still scattered, not linked together. South Korean farmers told the author about three reasons of such situation. Firstly, the peasant households that stay in rural areas and the peasant households that leave the rural areas are distributed randomly. Such randomness is the main reason causing the peasant households that stay in rural areas unable to purchase the lands linked together. Secondly, although there is a land market, yet it cannot be guaranteed that each peasant household gets equally sufficient information for each land transaction; this enables land transaction to be incidental to certain degree, and influences linking of the lands. Thirdly, land transaction between which peasant households is closely related to the relationship between the peasant households. That is to say, with respect to whom the peasants leaving the rural areas will sell their lands to, price is not the only determinant factor. Such human relations will also influence the linking of lands.

1.3.5 Direction of the collective ownership of rural land

(1) The relationship between collective economy and market economy

In many cases, collective economy may adopt the methods of market economy, i.e. market economy and collective economy are inclusive to a great degree. But in essence, market economy is contract economy, collective economy is cooperative economy. The reason why market economy is contract economy lies in economic exchanges in market economy mainly between strangers, the economic exchanges between strangers must be guaranteed by contract with legal effect. Economic exchanges in collective economy mainly occur between acquaintances, the economic exchanges between acquaintances may be guaranteed not only by contract with legal effect, but also by mutual trust based on blood lineage and geography. In this respect, collective economy is not complete market economy.

Scope of economic intercourse of the peasant households always becomes larger and larger. With the expansion of intercourse scope, the proportion of trading with acquaintances will become smaller and smaller, the proportion of trading with strangers will become larger and larger. So in the long term, importance of market economy will increase with the increase of economic development level, meanwhile importance of collective economy will decrease with the increase of economic development level.

Another reason of the decreased importance of collective economy: in a market system with many defects, cooperation is specific measures of the peasants in a weak position to resist the exploitation of industrial and commercial capital. With the increasingly fierce market competition, market information becomes more and more sufficient, market defects are overcome gradually, the importance of collective economy will decrease. This is also an important reason why cooperatives in developed countries increasingly tend to be incorporated.

(2) The relationship between household management and collective management

At the development stage when economy is underdeveloped, management scale of peasant households is generally too small, functions and capabilities at household management level are very limited, here supplemented by collective management level, it is obviously better than single household management level.

Of course, even if at this stage, household management is also a fundamental management level, collective management is a supplementary management level. Before the reform and opening, fundamental role of household management level was denied completely only single collective management level existed, went to an extreme; after the reform and opening, complementary role of collective management level is basically denied, only single household management level exists, goes to an extreme again. In fact, household management level and collective management level may be inclusive, complementary and coexist. Historically, collective actions of the peasant households on the village level, for example, peasant households participate in the construction and maintenance of irrigation facilities jointly, always exist. The assets developed by such collective actions are the assets of "collective economy".

In the process of economic development, most peasant households will leave agriculture gradually. Since non-agriculturization speed of the peasants exceeds non-agriculturization speed of rural land greatly, peasant households that stay in rural areas will have gradually expanded management scale of rural land, functions at household management level will be improved gradually, and capabilities will be enhanced step by step, corresponding to such changes, the role of collective management level will decrease gradually.

1.3.6 Suggestions for countermeasures against adjusting the realization form of collective ownership of rural land

It may be seen from literature that, most discussions on effective realization form of the collective ownership of rural land regard the maintaining of existing land property structure as basic precondition, those discussed are the things that should be decided by the peasants independently. In fact, for those things that should be decided by the peasants independently, it is unnecessary for the decision-making level to go beyond their duties and meddle in others' affairs. Decision-making level should do the following: analyze the defects of existing land property structure, discuss operable improvement methods on this basis, so that peasants may have more flexible options for independent decision-making. Following the analysis of this thinking, adjustment should be made for existing land property structure in the following three aspects.

(1) Add land equity

Compared with land contract right, land equity is obviously more normalized and more precise from the viewpoint of jurisprudence, anyone could understand it correctly without any ambiguity. From the viewpoint of economics, this concept is obviously clearer and more reasonable. Contracting and contract awarding are a pair of concepts. General practice of rural collective economic organizations to exercise the right to award contract is that, all members should have equal right to compete for contract, the contract winner will obtain the right to contract. According to such practice, generally it is impossible for all collective members to get equal right to contract. Actually it is the land equity that was distributed equally as per population and labor force at the early stage of reform, use of the term "the right to contract" while avoiding "land equity" mainly intended to reduce political sensitivity, so that common understanding might be reached on the agrarian reform at the decision-making level, this fully embodies the wisdom of peasants and agents of change.

The right to contract has become an idiom in agricultural policies in China. In order to maintain continuity of policy expressions, a secure method is to reserve the concept of the right to contract, at the same time, to add land equity in land property structure. The reason: contract management right is divided into the right to contract and management right according to the existing land property structure, economic substance of land contract right is land equity. As it is, use of the cognitively ambiguous right to contract[①] to reject the unambiguous land equity is not a good choice. With land equity, members of a collective economic organization always have equal right to compete for the contracted management of collective assets, the initially equal land equity will not vary with the transfer of management right, the initially equal right to contract will vary with the transfer of management right and become unequal. Such property right structure is favorable to keep effective allocation of collective assets.

(2) Change the land contract right in physical form to the land equity in value form

At the early stage of "all-round responsibility system", all peasant households managed their contracted lands. Here land contract right must correspond to specific plots in physical form. Now, more and more peasant households no longer manage their contracted lands, concern the lands from production function to property function, the conditions for changing land contract right in physical form to land equity in value form are basically met.

---

① The winning member of a rural collective economic organization obtains the right to contract in general situations. It is also the case in "Contract after Rental" of rural land, the winner obtains the right to contract. Since the members of a rural collective economic organization have a very rare opportunity to obtain equal right to contract, so use of the right to contract to embody the land property right of collective economic organization members is not of general significance.

(3) Change the production right of specific land to income right of specific land equity

With more and more peasant households no longer manage their contracted lands, peasant households that stay in agriculture objectively have the opportunities to expand management scale. Expansion of management scale will inevitably involve land consolidation; in order to promote land consolidation, the land production right originally assigned to peasant households needs to be changed to land income right. Such adjustment is of great significance for increasing the efficiency of agricultural production, increasing international competitiveness of agriculture in China.

2. Safeguard the peasants' rights and interests in land according to law

The peasants' rights and interests in land, include the rights and interests in collective agricultural land and collective construction land. Comparatively speaking, the rights and interests in collective agricultural land are defined clearly, while the rights and interests in collective construction land are not defined very clearly. Therefore, emphasis of further reform should be placed on rural collective construction land, especially the construction land under rural collective management.

2.1 Evaluation of the policy for rights and interests in rural land

In reality, problems exist in the protection, management and realization of the rights and interests in rural land. Existing policy is designed surrounding how to realize income from the transfer of land rights; systematic, consistency deviations exist. The development process is the process in which contribution rate of human capital to economic growth increases continuously. In this process, enhancing capability of the peasants continuously is critical to increase the income of peasant households continuously. Since increase of the peasant income mainly comes from capability improvement of the peasants, the role of income from transfer of land rights will become more and more limited. Objectively speaking, collective economic organizations and peasant households concern more about the protection of rights and interests in rural land, local government concerns more about the transaction of rights and interests in rural land, i.e. the interests and dependency of local government on the transactions of rural collective agricultural land, construction land under collective management, peasant house sites and houses are significantly higher than that of rural collective economic organizations and peasant households.

Clear definition of the rights of collective economic organization and peasant households in the design of rural land transaction system is very meaningful and very important. But it must be pointed out that, rural land transaction system serves some collective economic organizations and peasants at any time, while rural land protection and management system serves all collective economic organizations and peasant households at any time, therefore, the design of rural land protection and management system is more meaningful and more important, must be promoted with priority.

Stable purpose and ownership of rural land is very important. This is an important reason why all countries in the world implement land purpose planning and restrict rural land transactions. For peasants, transfer of land equity could really bring big gains to them instantaneously, however, few peasants are moved for this. This judgment may be based on the peasants generally rejecting the policy of land for identity. Gains of the peasants from transfer of land management right are stable and limited, yet the contribution to income growth is one-off, could not increase income continuously. It is no secret that, industrial and commercial capital in Chinese cities is keen on obtaining rural land, not to be engaged in agricultural production, nor for grain growing, but looking for the opportunities to change the purpose of rural land. Therefore, rural land transaction should not be uncontrolled; attention should not be paid only to the short-term benefits from reshuffling of rural land ownership while neglecting the risk for breaking up such stability, nor policy-related incentive may be given for reshuffling of rural land ownership. In a word, the truly needed pattern is that peasants rely on capability improvement to increase income continuously, the misunderstanding that peasants rely on transfer of rural land rights to increase income must be abandoned.

It is analyzed that, the problems of the peasants' exercise of rights and interests in land exist in two aspects. We should deepen the reform with respect to the infringement of peasants' legitimate rights and interests, eliminate these barriers thoroughly, and strengthen management with respect to the peasants' excessive exercise of rights and interests, remove these barriers completely.

2.1.1 Policy deviation that influences the rights and interests of rural collective economic organizations

(1) The impact of government monopoly policy on the peasants' rights and interests in land

The peasants' legitimate rights and interests in land are mainly infringed by government. Government becomes the only subject of rural collective land acquisition by virtue of the institutional arrangement of monopoly in primary land market; it may obtain permanent ownership of the land from rural collective economic organizations at the price of land-use right for many years, then sell the land-use right for specific years at the price of land ownership in marketing modes of bid invitation,auction and listing. Such practice obtaining huge amount of land price difference by virtue of monopoly power must be reformed. Government should be dedicated to management responsibility, collect taxes related to land transactions according to law, guide enterprises to cooperate with rural collective economic organizations, so that it is unnecessary for the enterprises to pay huge amount of land price, rural collective economic organizations could obtain permanent land equity income, thus enterprise products and services could have stronger market competitiveness.

(2) The impact of alternative government policy on the deduction right of rural collective economic organizations

After "all-round responsibility system" was implemented, collective ownership of rural land has been realized by exercising the deduction right. Whereas many problems existed in collective reductions, after the government cancelled agricultural tax, collective reduction system was not executed any more. The alternative measures involve government issuing subsidies to village cadres, providing basic public services required by rural communities. Advantages of such alternative include alleviation of peasants' burden, resolution of the conflict between village cadres and villagers; yet two problems are generated, firstly, interfere the implementation of villager autonomy system, secondly, deprive collective economic organizations of the right of income from management right of the contracted land. With respect to the substitution of government responsibilities for the responsibilities of community members, its advantage of alleviating the burden of peasants is visible at once, however, its disadvantge will not disappear because not exposed yet.

(3) The impact of excessive intervention policy on the rural collective economic organizations to exercise rights

"Case-by-case" is a good system, but due to the provision of no more than

15 Yuan per capita for each financing, village cadres are unwilling to attempt to use the "case-by-case" system just for a financing amount of tens of thousand Yuan. Especially when many alternative measures are available, village cadres will inevitably prefer to seek help from the government, from the entrepreneurs, rather than from the villagers. In fact, "case-by-case" matters should be decided by village meeting or villagers' representative meeting, it is completely unnecessary for the government to add provisions such as no more than 15 Yuan per capita for each financing.

2.1.2 Deviation of the peasants' excessive exercise of rights and interests in land caused by loose management

Actual problems not only include infringement of rights and interests in rural land, but also excessive exercise of rights and interests due to loose management of land purpose by the government. Specifially in the following three aspects.

(1) Non-agriculturization problem of rural land

The land purpose planning in China is not rigorous, may be adjusted once per year. That is to say, local governments may formulate land purpose adjustment plan every year, as long as approved by land authorities, the plan may serve as legal basis to adjust land purpose planning. Let alone non-strict land purpose management, even land purpose adjustment plan might be broken through occasionally. So in reality, cultivated land might be changed to non-agricultural land in the urbanization process, and might be leased by companies in the name of developing modern agriculture, then changed to non-agricultural land in various ways.

(2) Inefficiency problem of rural land

In order to eliminate the abandoned land, institutional arrangement entitling rural collective to take back the land abandoned for years is made in some places. Collective economic organization may only judge cultivation or no cultivation by the contracted households, could not judge whether investment strength of the contracted households meets the requirements. So some peasant households that do not want to waive land contract right cultivate the land to prevent collective economic organization from taking back the contract management right, rather than cultivating for the purpose of income from the land, so agricultural production behaviors without concern on efficiency appear. Such behaviors are caused by untight rural land management policy of the government after all.

(3) Unsustainable problem of rural land

Although both food safety and environmental safety are national strategic goals, yet the goal of food safety is significantly superior to the goal of environmental safety in actual operations. This is the main reason of excessive use of agrochemicals such as fertilizers, pesticides, plastic film. For such problems, do not reprehend low quality of the peasants too much, but introspect agriculture subsidy policy of the government deeply. Because excessive use of chemicals in agricultural production is more closely related to the excessive production subsidies issued by government.

2.1.3 Evaluation of the government land policy

(1) Rural land

As a whole, small peasant households are still dominant in the agriculture of China. In recent years, some large households with appropriate management scale, that adopt modern agricultural technology appear in rural areas, they benefit old and weak groups, part-time peasant households in the communities by means of pooling of land as shares, peasants join cooperatives. Such win-win cooperation mode worthy for popularization is closely related to the policy guidance of government at all levels. We should also see that, in some places, government utilizes public resources to build large households, even support urban industrial and commercial capital to enter agriculture field, yet numerous small farms could not get any support. It must be pointed out that, transfer of rural land management right should be a rational choice of the peasants, should be the result of market allocation of resources. The development of appropriate management scale requires long time, please do not be anxious for success, so never force the peasants to transfer land management right by administrative means, that will infringe the rights and interests of small peasant households in land. For urban industrial and commercial capital entering agriculture field, protect their legal rights and interests, and inhibit their encroachment on the rights and interests of small peasant households in land. Policy orientation in the future should: adhere to the fundamental position of household management, develop family farms with self-sustainability or land stock cooperatives, increase the income from rural land equity gradually by pooling land management right to large households or cooperatives that could create higher benefits.

(2) Commercial construction land

An invisible market of rural collective construction land already exists for 30 years. Pilot transfer of government-dominated collective construction land in market has been carried out in 22 provinces and districts in China, local regulations for the transfer of collective construction land have also been promulgated in some provinces and cities. Now experience should be summarized carefully, and law should be formulated for collective land marketing on this basis, rather than still at pilot stage.

Appropriate policy orientation: the government should substitute land planning management system for land acquisition system, protect basic rights and land increment income of the land under collective management. Break up the monopoly of government on primary land market, establish open, competitive, unified and orderly land market, bring the decisive role of market allocation of resources into play. Land planning management intends to coordinate the relationship between near term interests, local interests and long-term interests, global interests of land use. It complements the development of land market, is not a substitution. Land purpose planning management intends to prevent market defects, and subsequent serious consequence.

Explore the cooperation mode of rural collective land in equity form with industry capital and financial capital, enable persistence of the peasants' land income on the one hand, iron out the land cost to be paid by industry capital, financial capital in the industrialization, urbanization process on the other hand. Develop balancing mechanism in rural collective economic organizations, let common members grasp control power and residual claim of land increment income to certain degree.

(3) Peasant house sites

Management of peasant house sites is not solved well all the time. Current main task is to implement the policy of one house site for one household properly. Specific reform orientation: innovate realization form of the usufructuary right of peasant house sites and the property right of peasant houses; set bottom line for the transfer of house property right, guarantee housing security of the peasants. Mortgagers must commit that, they will not apply for new house sites from village committee after housing mortgage, so as to prevent immoral behaviors. Assignee of the house property right should pay infrastructure fee.

2.2 Safeguard the peasants' rights and interests in land according to law

Infringement of the rights and interests of rural collective economic organizations and peasant households in land is one of the most prominent problems. It influences long-term economic interests of the peasants, influences rural social stability, and influences ruling foundation of the Communist Party of

China. Such problems must be solved relying on the force of laws and regulations. Compelling force of laws and regulations must be applied to inhibit encroachment of strong groups on the rights and interests of vulnerable groups in land comprehensively.

2.2.1 Safeguard collective ownership of rural land according to law

The so-called safeguarding collective ownership of rural land according to law means to utilize the rights conferred by the Constitution and other laws to safeguard collective ownership of rural land, ensure contract management right of the peasants not to be violated.

2.2.2 Normalize the behaviors of government and officials according to law

A prominent problem in reality is that government departments and officials do not handle affairs according to the administrative license law, they do some things not permitted by laws and regulations, infringe the peasants' rights and interests in land. Therefore, administrative rules according to law must be reiterated and executed strictly. Government and officials at whichever level shall not do anything unallowed by laws and regulations. At the same time, laws and regulations should be utilized to safeguard the rights and interests of rural collective economic organizations and peasant households in land, especially to inhibit individual government officials and urban industrial and commercial capital from encroaching the land of rural collective economic organizations cooperatively.

2.2.3 Normalize the behaviors of village cadres according to law

Another prominent phenomenon in reality is that village cadres dominate collective land property right at will, infringe the peasants' rights and interests in land. These behaviors are unlawful, may be inhibited completely according to law. Village cadres often act absurdly under the shelter of individual government officials. These patrons should also be handled according to law.

2.2.4 Improve the laws and regulations to safeguard peasants' rights and interests in land

Although many existing laws and regulations involve the rights and interests in rural land,yet operability is not strong, coverage is not wide enough. In order to protect the peasants' rights and interests in land against infringement, coordinate the political, social, economic, cultural relationship with the rights and interests in land, laws and regulations must be further improved to safeguard the peasants' rights and interests in land.

2.3 Policy suggestions for safeguarding the peasants' rights and interests in land

2.3.1 Change rural land from physical capital to equity capital

Right verification of rural land should be based on the right verification in physical form, yet should not be confined to the right verification in physical form, because such right verification mode is unfavorable for land consolidation, also unfavorable for actual land operator to obtain land increment income.

Definition of property right in physical form is the most simple, clearest property right definition method, yet not the only one. For example, water rights, since definition method of property right in physical form is unavailable, alternative method is figured out. Therefore, water rights always refer to the rights to use specific water flow fraction or water flow. If definition of grassland property right adopts the most simple property right definition method, there will be too many fences,[①] which damage the integrity of grassland ecosystem , so a property right definition method of grazing rights is created. Specifically, reasonable grazing capacity of a specific meadow is divide by the area of specific meadow to obtain the grazing rights of unit grassland area, then multiplied by the contracted meadow area of each herdsman household to obtain the grazing rights of each herdsman household. The transfer of grazing rights is obviously simpler than the transfer of meadow. For cultivated land, determine production capacity of specific plot (mean annual yield) , although it is more difficult than defining four boundaries of a specific plot on the map, yet this is very important. With this, rural land is changed from physical capital to equity capital, equity capital is comparable, thus rural land capital is comparable, and may flow just as financial capital.

① Here it means too many fences or fences per household, rather than no need of fences. To keep integrity of the grassland ecosystem, the fewer fences, the better.

2.3.2 Promote the reform of rural collective land shareholding system

Collective ownership of rural land needs insistence, and needs reform. Reform aims to better insistence. The reform of rural collective land is oriented to promote shareholding system.

(1) The role of pooling of rural land as shares

Firstly, solve sidelining issue of agriculture effectively. If peasants have land equity, could obtain land income in the form of dividend distribution, they could leave agriculture completely, enter cities to seek employment opportunities, so as to quicken the transition of urban-rural dual structure. Secondly, overcome negative impact of land fragmentation effectively. Realize mass production and industrialization of agricultural production, increase production efficiency of rural land, increase income of the peasants. Thirdly, increase flexibility of land occupation and transfer. Transition of land occupation in physical form to occupation in value form could increase the flexibility of land occupation, the flexibility of land transfer and the convenience of land consolidation.

(2) Pooling principles of rural land as shares

Firstly, land equity has legal guarantee. The state should formulate laws and regulations as soon as possible to provide system guarantee for land equity. This is fundamental work to guide land shareholding reform and ensure normalization of land equity. Secondly, rights and interests in land have contract guarantee. There are risks in agricultural production. In order to dissolve the risks that might impair the peasants' interests and endanger rural stability, insurance and reinsurance measures must be taken to ensure peasant households with land equity not to lose their land property income because of the risks in agricultural production. Thirdly, pooling of land as shares meets the peasants' willingness. Government should guarantee land shareholding reform not to violate the peasants' willingness, not infringe the peasants' interests, not violate national policy.

(3) Overall thinking of the shareholding system reform

Overall thinking of the shareholding system reform for rural collective land: the reform should be promoted in existing institutional framework, so that institutional change cost is small, income uncertainty is low, risks could be controlled. The shareholding system reform of rural collective land in China started from 1992, was tried in many places in these years. Now both excellent foundation and experience worthy of reference are available for this reform, all conditions are met.

Preliminary conception: take village or village group as unit to establish land stock cooperative. Stock cooperative has three types of equity shares, namely, peasant household shares, collective shares and corporate shares; runs in the principles of voluntariness, equality and mutual benefit, and according to the rules of fund co-financing, property co-ownership, co-decision-making, risk sharing and profit sharing. Land stock cooperative has articles of association, council, board of supervisors and member conference, has various certificates required for independent legal entity, has special bank account. Members have the rights to join the cooperative voluntarily and exit the cooperative freely, the right to vote and right to be elected, beneficial right of shares, employment priority, wage assignment right, residual claim, as well as the right to learn the truth, appraisal rights of development plan, financial statement, assets management scheme. Rules for excess profit in a progressive way, and rules for dismiss if work unsatisfactory to above half of the members are applicable to the council members. The members execute participants sharing rules to increase the sense of involvement of members, and remold the sense of identity and sense of belonging of the peasants to the collective.

2.3.3 Optimization of macropolicy environment for land system reform

Optimization of macro environment for land system reform and safeguarding income of the peasant collective from property are more important, more critical than the clarification of land property right. Main optimization contents of macro environment for land system reform: further return rights to peasants and empower them, create conditions for peasants to select property right form independently (including occupation, use, income, transfer etc) , safeguard the peasants' right to learn the truth of information, prevent malicious information distortion; improve democratic system at the basic level, clear legal appeal channels, safeguard fairness and justice.

3. Development of collective economy

3.1 The significance of developing collective economy

Through institutional evolution for over three decades, diversified economic sectors coexist in rural China and are developed jointly. For over three decades, collective economy is always one of the organic components of rural economy. Collective economy is emphasized on policy orientation, intends to solve backward development of collective economy, not to suppress the development of other economic sectors, nor create conditions for agricultural economy to transit to the ownership by the whole people.

3.1.1 Analysis of the influencing factors of collective action performance

The process of human development is accompanied with collective action. Some people would like to take collective action, because the performance of collective action is better than the performance of individual action. Some people are unwilling to take collective action, because the performance of collective action is not as good as the performance of individual action. The performance of individual action is stable, the performance of collective action might be higher than or lower than the performance of individual action, reasons can only be found from the supervision and incentive system of collective action. In brief, if the supervision and incentive system is designed properly, the performance of collective action will be superior to the performance of individual action, if supervision and incentive system is designed improperly, the performance of collective action will not be as good as the performance of individual action. Scholars have discussed such problems deeply.

Amartya K. Sen published an article in 1966[①], in which he demonstrated a conclusion that the labor enthusiasm of workers in cooperative farms would be higher than that in individual farms, main measures to achieve this effect is to eliminate external negative incentives.

Olson divided collective interests into inclusive interests and exclusive interests, the former means that collective members are mutually inclusive when pursuing individual interests, for example, collective members require a purchaser to give a higher purchase price of agricultural products; the latter means that collective members are mutually exclusive when pursuing individual interests, for example, in case of limited purchase, the competition between peasant households is exclusive. According to the game theory, inclusive situation corresponds to positive-sum game, exclusive situation corresponds to zero-sum game. Whereas collective action of prisoner's dilemma might appear even in inclusive situation, Olson emphasized that, the selective incentive impartial in the dispensation of reward and punishment must be designed for collective members; in order to overcome incomplete information equivalence in real world, scale of the collective should not be too large.

Lin Yifu analyzed the relationship between incentive, supervision and collective economy performance. He pointed out that, the principle for peasant households to join the commune voluntarily, and exit freely was respected before 1958. During the people community movement, the principle of voluntary join and free exit was denied. From the view point of game theory, voluntary join and free exit correspond to repeated games, commune members may make a better choice for themselves by joining and exiting the commune; the compulsory join and unpermitted exit correspond to one-time game, commune members could not improve their situations by making choices. Blind expansion of cooperation scale further aggravates the difficulties of supervision and incentive.

To sum up, the advantages and disadvantages of collective action performance mainly depend on the design of supervision and incentive system. While good design of supervision and incentive system must respect collective wisdom and common choice of the peasants. Therefore, the indispensable fundamental work for collective economy to get on the right track is to let the peasants decide economic cooperation mode, design microscopic supervision and incentive system jointly.

---

① Amartya K.Sen, "A possibility theorem on majority decisions", Econometrica, 34,2,1966, pp. 491-499.

3.1.2 Analysis on the necessity and possibility of developing rural collective economy

The data from the Ministry of Agriculture show that, by the end of 2009, total collective assets at village level was 1.6 trillion Yuan in 617,700 villages of 30 provinces in China (except Tibet) , excluding resources assets such as land, mountain forest, water surface, grassland. Good management of this part of collective assets is of extreme importance for enhancing the strength of collective economy, public service capability of rural communities, improving community infrastructure, regulating village appearance and improving eco-environment, then further enhancing cohesiveness, charisma and influence of the community. To truly realize this, backward development of collective economy must be reversed as soon as possible.

In the Decision of CPC Central Committee on A Number of Important Issues concerning the Rural Reform and Development, collective management was placed in the same important position as household management, cooperative management and business management for the first time. This strategic deployment will promote the development of collective economy effectively.

It is no secret that, extra small scale agricultural management mode does not influence the peasant households to get adequate food and clothing, however, it is really difficult to cope with marketization, industrialization and global challenges. This is an important reason to guide the peasants in cooperation and development of rural collective economy. Survey shows that, the peasants both "expect" and "fear" the development of collective economy, they expect collective economy to provide services, but fear only assuming responsibilities, no enjoyment of services. So the development of collective economy should not follow the old way of "gathering" and evil ways of depriving the peasants' interests, but should deepen the reform according to actual situation of villages, improve supervision and incentive system, should find a new way of members with equal rights, co-ownership of assets by shares, contribution-based interest sharing, relying on the peasants and serving the peasants.

Collective economy is the product of rural socialist transformation. Collective economy at village level still exists although it has been affected by agricultural "all-round responsibility system", restructuring of township and village enterprises and cancellation of "three deductions and five charges" in over three decades, the peasants still accept collective economy. The investigation conducted by Zhongnan

University of Economics and Law shows that,[①] 80.9% of the peasants surveyed thought that collective property right should be safeguarded practically, 82.9% of the peasants surveyed thought that organization mode of collective economy should be improved, 73.6% of the peasants surveyed expected tax preference to collective economy.

The peasant households surveyed thought that, village collective played an active role in the following aspects: strengthen the construction of public welfare undertakings such as road, water conservancy, potable water (98.1%) , improve rural culture, education, environmental sanitation facilities (92.1%) , appropriate subsidies for members (peasants) who lost land or have no land (47.0%) , provide social security (medical treatment, pension, unemployment etc) funds (76.6%) , provide services for the contracted management of peasant households (73.6%) , provide local employment opportunities for collective members (68.8%) . At the same time, all of the peasant households surveyed hoped their village collective economic organizations to play a greater role, i.e. there is a gap between the role of village collective and the expectation of peasant households.

Almost all of the peasant households surveyed accepted the integration of ollective economic organization and villagers committee, they worried that additional collective economic organization might increase management cost. And thought that special person should be designated to take charge of economic development in the villagers committee. With respect to the effect of villagers committee (village group) to exercise economic function, 61.3% of the peasant households surveyed thought "excellent", 26% of the peasant households surveyed thought "general", only 3.9% of the peasant households surveyed thought "poor". This shows that it is not completely infeasible for the villagers committee to exercise economic function on behalf of rural collective economic organizations.

Over half of the peasant households surveyed thought that, village collective shall be entitled to charge certain amount of cultivated land contracting fee, use right transfer fee of house sites and private plots (hills) (50.3%) , decide the distribution of private plots (hills) (51%) , and decide the distribution of house sites (67.7%) .

With respect to the impact of basic-level government on village collective

① The subject group investigated 72 villages in 12 provinces, namely, Hubei, Shangdong, Heilongjiang, Shanxi, Shaanxi, Henan, Sichuan, Guizhou, Guangdong, Hebei, Anhui, Jiangsu Province, of which famous villages and common villages accounted for about 50% each. (data source: Chen Xiaojun, Gao Fei, Geng Zhuo: Empirical Survey on Rural Collective Economy in China to Realize Structure of the Law Effectively--A Survey Report from 12 Provinces, Studies in Law and Business, 6th Issue, 2012) economic organizations to exercise function: 72.3% of the peasant households surveyed thought no improper intervention, 18.1% of the peasant households surveyed thought a little improper intervention, only 7.7% of the peasant households surveyed thought more improper intervention.

The survey of 300 peasant household questionnaires conducted by Zhu Youzhi et al in ten villages of five towns and townships in Hunan Province also shows that: 47% of the peasant households thought their villages or groups had collective assets (including land, mountain forest, houses, workshops, water surface etc) . In order to increase income source of the collective, 50.4% of peasant households would like to gather a part of individually contracted cultivated land and forest land as collective assets of the villages and groups; 25.2% of the peasant households disagreed, 24.4% of the peasant households did not give definite reply. 59.3% of the peasant households would like to gather a part of individually contracted cultivated land and forest land as collective assets of their villages and groups in the way of pooling land as shares.①

3.1.3 The reason of slow development of rural collective economy

Rural collective economy has been developed very slowly for over three decades, many villages are in "empty shell" state. Main reasons of the extremely slow development of rural collective economy are analyzed as follows:

Firstly, the development foundation of rural collective economy is extruded. After "all-round responsibility system" was implemented, collective assets of many villages were almost separated out, number of villages truly keeping collective management level with increment of collective assets dropped sharply, but most villages relied on "three deductions and five charges" for public affairs of the villages. If "three deductions and five charges" reserved an element of collective economy, then this element of collective economy did not exist after the reform of rural taxes.

Secondly, development conditions of rural collective economy are immature. Peasant households have different element structures, for example, some have more lands, some have more labor forces, some have skills, these are prerequisites for the cooperation of peasant households. The promotion of "all-round responsibility system" enhances homogeneity of the peasant households. Through years of division of work and occupation among the peasant households, and

① Zhu Youzhi, Xiao Wei: "Second Leap" of Collective Economy is the Only Way of New Rural Construction, *Exploring*, 2007(11).

differentiation of the peasants, such conditions become better and better.

Thirdly, underconfidence of the peasant households in the development of rural collective economy. Before the reform, the people's commune system did not bring any advantage to the peasant households hard to give up; after the reform, income distribution of rural collective economy is unfair, the peasants' obligation to submit various deductions is asymmetrical with the sharing of welfare, so many peasants lack of confidence in the development of collective economy.

Fourthly, incomplete systems, nonstandard management. Due to lax management, imperfect supervision, general chaos in bookkeeping at village level, collective assets, resources and funds suffer from severe loss and waste, village cadres often violate the laws and disciplines etc.

Fifthly, cadres and the masses still have the ideas of "wait, depend, request". The weaker the collective economy is, the more serious the "wait, depend, request" ideas become. The concept of relying on government restricts the development of collective economy at village level seriously.

3.1.4 Favorable conditions for the development of collective economy

It is analyzed that, three favorable conditions are available to develop collective economy:

(1) The growth of local able persons

The largest change in over three decades since the reform and opening in rural China is the emergence of a number of local able persons. They would like to fulfill responsibilities and make contributions to the development of their hometown. This group is the talent base to develop collective economy. The role of such persons must be given into full play in the development of collective economy, and their requirements should be met.

(2) Access of collective construction land to the market

Under the action of market mechanism, the allocation of rural collective construction land will be optimized, the increased utilization efficiency of rural construction land will vitalize rural collective economy, and bring more fortune to the peasant collective. This is resource base for the development of collective economy. The development of collective economy must fully utilize this base.

(3) The environment of rural revolution and peasant differentiation

With more and more peasants employed in non-agricultural sectors, the conditions of land transfer, pooling of land as shares and land fragmentation will get better and better. Such changes will promote the development of modern agriculture and enhancement of agricultural competitiveness on the one hand, and will promote the development of collective economy on the other hand. This is macro environment for the development of collective economy. This environment must be fully utilized for the development of collective economy.

3.2 Legal status of rural collective economic organizations

3.2.1 Optimize the development environment of collective economic organizations from the improvement of relevant laws and regulations

(1) Guarantee the development of rural collective economy from improvement of legal and regulatory system

The development of rural collective economy requires the support of laws and regulations, this is not only the view of scholars, but also the view of peasant households. The survey result of peasant households shows that: 77.7% and 80.7% of the peasant households surveyed thought that, village collective economy needed legal support in "improvement of organization mode", "practical safeguarding of collective property right "respectively. In order to make clear legal status of rural collective economic organizations, government departments have done many works. According to incomplete statistics, about 30 laws, 40 regulations of the State Council, 101 regulations of the ministries and commissions involve rural collective economic organizations. However, relevant legal and regulatory system is still defective, needs to be further improved.

(2) Reconstruct rural collective economic organization into business corporation from improvement of the management structure

According to law, the real property and movable property collectively owned by the peasants belong to collective members jointly. Rural collective economic organization is the property owner of rural collective assets. Function of the rural collective economic organization as property owner of rural collective assets is to manage land and other rural collective assets, seek benefits for the collective organization members. In order to facilitate rural collective economic organization to carry out business activities in a better way, collective economic organization should reconstruct and improve its management structure to become business corporation with cooperative enterprise features.

(3) Cultivate joint-stock enterprise in rural community from the improvement of "three-capital" shareholding procedure

Community joint-stock system is the reform direction of rural collective economic organization. The so-called community joint-stock system is based on rural collective economic organization, tied by collective land ownership, all or part of the community collective property is converted to shares and quantified to the qualified collective members. Organizational framework is established with reference to the management structure of shareholding system, include shareholder congress, council and board of supervisors, democratic management and sharing profits according to contributions are implemented.

Community joint-stock system is the result of induced institutional change. Although existing rural community joint-stock system needs to be improved, yet it has actually become an effective realization form of collective economy. Therefore, rural community joint-stock enterprise should be confirmed and normalized at the legal level in the future.

3.2.2 Quicken the legislation of rural collective economic organizations

(1) Normalize "three-capital" management procedure of rural collective economic organizations

Firstly, rural collective economic organization and villagers autonomous organization should deal with their relationship properly. Secondly, rural collective economic organizations should draw on the cumulative experience in domestic and foreign development practices in aspects of rural collective assets, fund, resource management. Thirdly, basic-level government shall be liable to provide instructions, supervision and services for the development of rural collective economy, but should not participate in the management directly.

(2) Normalize registration certificate procedure of rural collective economic organizations

Firstly, rural collective assets management department at and above county level should be responsible for the registration certificate of rural collective economic organizations. Specific works in two aspects: normalize the name of rural collective economic organizations; verify the assets of rural collective economic organizations. Secondly, registration certificate. This is a prerequisite for rural collective economic organizations to transact industrial and commercial registration and tax registration.

(3) Determine business corporation position of rural collective economic organizations

Firstly, reconstruct rural collective economic organizations comprehensively to meet the conditions of business corporation, become genuine legal subject for successful industrial and commercial registration and tax registration, carry out market economic activities actively. Secondly, encourage the rural collective economic organizations with collective assets up to certain scale to build joint-stock management structure. Thirdly, economic entities that have been transformed or have shares such as "limited liability company", are not in the scope to be adjusted by the legislation of rural collective economic organizations.

3.2.3 Legislative suggestions

It is advisable to formulate special Law of Rural Collective Economic Organizations to overcome the deviations of emphasizing legislation for management object of rural collective assets, yet neglecting the legislation for management subject of rural collective assets.

Rural collective economic organization belongs to Category 1 legal subject, belongs to civil basic system category, according to the Legislation Law of China, Standing Committee of the National People's Congress should formulate the Law of Rural Collective Economic Organizations, or National People's Congress should authorize the State Council to firstly formulate Regulations for Rural Collective Economic Organizations.

3.3 Overall thinking and policy suggestions for the development of rural collective economy

3.3.1 Overall thinking

Collective economy at village level has been developed in China for merely several decades, yet village governance model that integrates production and living lasts very long. The peasants accept such integrated model. Separation of collective economic organizations from villagers committee is surely the development direction,yet it is not a prerequisite for the development of collective economy, nor an urgent affair.

The development of rural collective economy should implement the principle of "rely on peasants, serve the peasants", promote the transition from able person model to institutional model. The following works should be done for the development of rural collective economy:

Firstly, choose appropriate management personnel. Broaden the visual field of candidates, improve employment standard, let talents who have high prestige in the masses, know operation and technologies, are skillful in management assume important tasks. A leader with new concept, high sense of responsibility, ability to handle affairs, devoted to contributions, trusted by the masses is especially important. With a good leader, innovative thinking, innovative route, innovative mechanism are available for the development of collective economy.

Secondly, return the right of rural collective property to people, empower the people. Property right of rural collective economic organizations is mainly manifested as land property right and enterprise property right. Verification of the property right is the precondition for operation of property right. Ambiguous collective property right should be changed by quantifying equity in the reform of property right system. In aspect of legislation, build legal environment, implement rights in practice, enhance resistance to improper, unlawful interference (especially of public power) .

Thirdly, increase economic management level of rural collective economic organizations. Firstly, strengthen "three-capital"(funds, assets and resources) management of collective economy practically. Specifially including, ascertain rural collective "three-capital" status, verify asset and capital, build supervision platform for "three-capital" information, promote institutionalization, normalization, informatization of rural collective "three-capital" management. Secondly, complete financial budget and final accounts, income management, expenditure approval, assets registration and other systems for rural collective. Thirdly, normalize contract award, lease, disposal procedures of rural collective assets, activate collective assets inventory, optimize collective assets increment, ensure rural collective economy to be developed in a healthy and rapid way.

Fourthly, increase the flexibility in project management mode of rural collective economic organizations. It is unnecessary for project management mode of rural collective economy to be unified, standardized. Villages should determine their management mode according to their respective resource endowment and features of the project, adapt measures to differing conditions in terms of locality,time and case, select contract or lease whichever is appropriate. Village collective economic organizations may innovate the management mode of rural collective economy, decide management mode and means independently in the preconditions of land for agricultural use, food security and ecological balance. With respect to the combination of centralization and decentralization of collective management and household management, household contract management is basic level, collective unified management is supplementary level. It must be pointed out that, the relationship between organization and members must be treated properly to realize the balancing and both consideration of member interests and organization interests for whichever mode adopted by rural collective economic organizations.

3.3.2 Policy suggestions

(1) Strengthen system construction, improve governance mechanism

The development of collective economy at village level requires: firstly, a good system. This is the most important. Both the advocacy of democratic management, and advocation of dedication awareness should be based on strict, perfect and symmetrical institutional restraints. Otherwise, bad money will drive out good and good money might be changed to bad money. Secondly, a good governance mechanism. This is crtical to ensure all efforts and works done towards the same goal.

(2) Increase support, lay a solid economic base

Firstly, provide policy support. Provide support and incentive to the collective economy development at village level, provide great support for tax, credit, electricity, land etc of collective economic project at village level. Secondly, increase financial support. Meet the requirements of normal operation at village level, increase the investment in public welfare facilities at village level, increase collective economic accumulation. Thirdly, emphasize project-promoting. Realize sound progress of collective economy at village level by providing "hematopoiesis" type support.

(3) Improve supervision and management, promote normalized operation

Firstly, normalize rural "three-capital" management. Strengthen the supervision of financial management at village level, prevent loss of collective assets. Secondly, complete the financial supervision mechanism at village level. Select and allocate excellent work personnel to town/township economic management stations, audit the financial works at village level periodically. Organization at village level should specify the use direction and principles of village collective funds strictly, bring the role of public financial management group, supervision group in the village into play, open financial income and expenditure at village level once per month, exercise strict control over various non-productive expenditures, manage and use collective funds well.

3.3.3 Tendencies to be prevented

In some developed areas, government provides funds to purchase agricultural machinery, build houses, village cadres gather the rural land of the whole village to develop family farms, cooperatives of mass, specialized and standardized production, such practices should not be advocated. There are three reasons: firstly, infringe the interests of small peasant households; secondly, invest the money of taxpayers to a few persons, incompliant with the principle of fairness; thirdly, lack of reproducibility. The development of modern agriculture is a progressive process, we have to prepare for a protracted war, prevent spoiling things by excessive enthusiasm.

This book is the result of a co-publication agreement between China Social Sciences Press (China) and Paths International Ltd (UK)

Title: Rural Land Reform, Peasants' Rights and the Collective Economy: Three Major Issues in China Agricultural Development
Author: Li Zhou, Ren Changqing
Translated by Li Yanqing
ISBN: 978-1-84464-567-1
Ebook ISBN: 978-1-84464-568-8

Paths International Ltd
www.pathsinternational.com
Published in the United Kingdom

CPSIA information can be obtained
at www.ICGtesting.com
Printed in the USA
LVHW062225180920
666521LV00001B/3

9 781844 645671